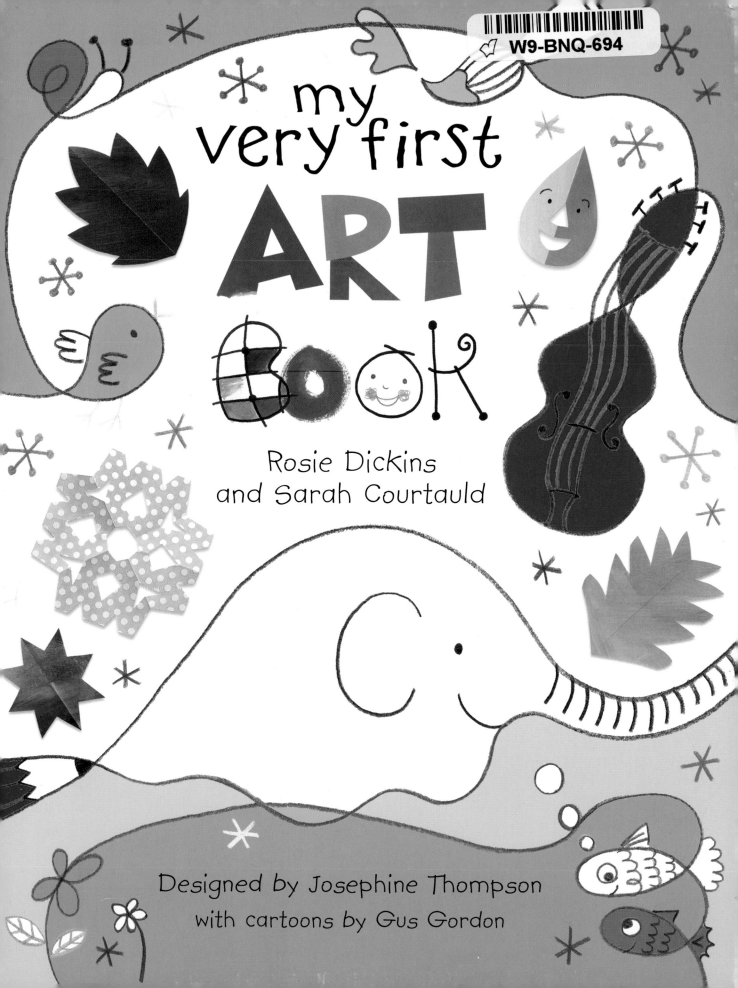

my very first ART Book

Rosie Dickins
and Sarah Courtauld

Designed by Josephine Thompson
with cartoons by Gus Gordon

Contents

This book is full of art to look at, and arty things to make and do. Start out by drawing, and then explore painting, printing, making paper cut-outs and making models.

Drawing

Printing

Painting

Cutting and pasting

Models

What you will need...

Pencils

Chalks

Paints

Brushes

Paper

Cardboard

Scissors

Fabric

Buttons

String

Sponges

Poster putty

Leaves

Non-toxic craft glue

Drawing and doodling

To start drawing, you just need
a pencil and a little imagination...

People at Night, Guided by Phosphorescent Tracks of Snails by Joan Miró

This artist used doodling to create funny
faces and strange, imaginary creatures
– and you can do this too.

Strange shapes

Start by doodling a long, wiggly line. Use other colors to turn your doodle into things.

Loopy animals

Try drawing animals like these without taking your pencil off the paper.

Scribble faces

Make a face out of just a few lines and shapes. Here are some ideas.

Drawing animals

You can draw animals by building them up from basic shapes such as circles, squares and triangles.

Elephant by Rembrandt van Rijn

An artist named Rembrandt drew this picture of an elephant. If you look carefully, you can see that the elephant's body is shaped like an oval and its legs are oblongs.

6

Elephant

Add lines for wrinkles

Draw an oval for the body. Add a circle for the head and four oblongs for legs.

Draw on a long curly trunk. Draw an ear and a tail.

Color in the elephant. Add a face and draw toenails on the feet.

Tiger

Draw a big oval for the body, and a smaller oval for the head. Add triangles for ears, oblongs for legs and a wavy tail.

Add blobs for feet.

Monkey

Start by drawing an oval for the body and a smaller oval for the head. Add arms, legs and a curly tail.

Add circles for ears.

Pony

Start with a large oval for the body and a small oval for the head, joined by a neck. Add stick legs.

Draw a mane and a tail.

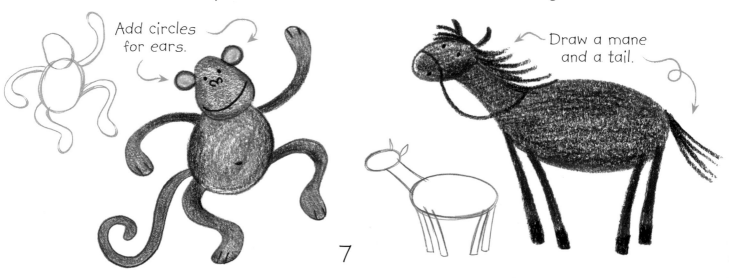

Coloring in

This woman's face is painted in all the colors of the rainbow. If you color in your drawings with really bright colors, it'll make them look more exciting.

Meduse by Alexei Jawlensky

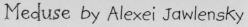

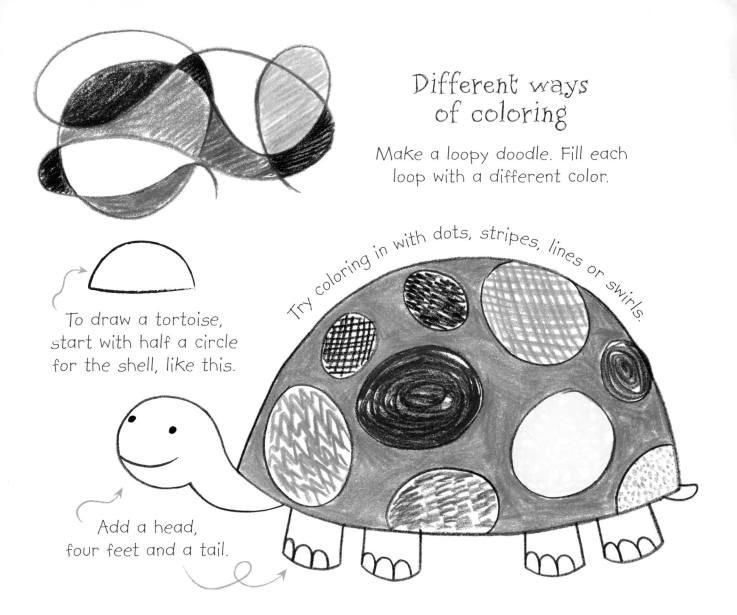

Different ways of coloring

Make a loopy doodle. Fill each loop with a different color.

Try coloring in with dots, stripes, lines or swirls.

To draw a tortoise, start with half a circle for the shell, like this.

Add a head, four feet and a tail.

Draw an outline of a fish, and add a few criss-cross lines over the top. Shade the sections in different colors.

Make a dog by scribbling with your pencil.

Scribble a rectangle for the dog's body, and then add a head, feet and a tail.

Smudgy scenes

Four Ballerinas by Edgar Degas

This artist used soft, blurry colors. You can use colored chalks to make your own smudgy picture.

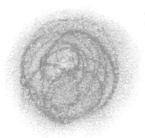

Draw a small circle with chalk. Rub the chalk with your fingertip to smudge it, like this.

You can blend two colors together by smudging them, like this.

Soft sheep

Draw curly lines to make a sheep's body, and smudge the chalk. Add a head, ears and legs.

Smudgy tree

Draw a tree in green and brown chalk, and smudge the green to look like leaves from a distance.

Pink rabbit

Draw a rabbit in chalk. Smudge the fur to make it look soft.

Chalky chicks

Draw some chicks in chalk. Smudge the feathers to make them look fluffy.

Bush Potato Dreaming by Victor Jupurrula Ross

This painting uses lots of dots
to create swirling patterns.

Playing with paint

There are lots of ways to apply paint. The dotty picture on the left was painted with brushes, but you can get a similar effect with fingers too.

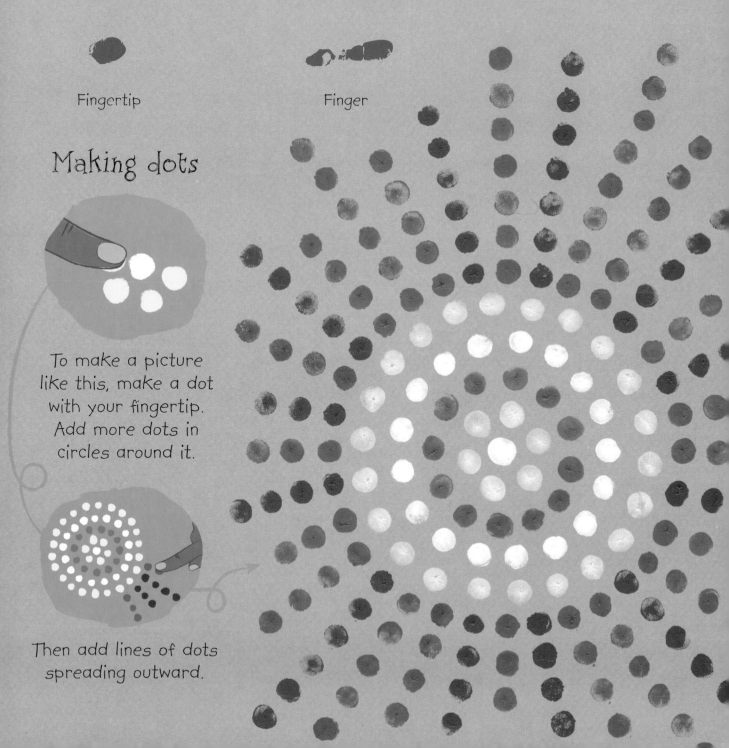

Fingertip

Finger

Making dots

To make a picture like this, make a dot with your fingertip. Add more dots in circles around it.

Then add lines of dots spreading outward.

Use black paper to fingerpaint an underwater scene, full of brightly colored sea creatures.

Big fish

Use your finger to paint a body. Add an eye, a fin and a tail. Use your fingertip to dot on scales all over the body.

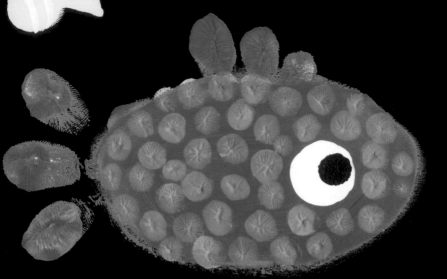

Loopy coral

With a brush, go around and around in loopy swirls, to make a coral reef.

Little fish

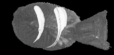

Fingerpaint a body, add a triangle for a tail, and then brush on stripes.

Sea turtle

Fingerpaint an oval shell-shape. Add round flippers, a head and tail. Dot on eyes and patterns on the shell.

Jellyfish

Fingerpaint a head. Dot on eyes with your little finger. Use a brush to add wavy tentacles and a mouth.

Octopus

Use your finger to paint a round head. Using your whole finger, print eight large tentacles. Paint a face with a brush and use your finger to add two red cheeks.

Wild colors

The artist who painted this picture of a sleeping fox has used bold colors. When you're painting, you can use any colors you like.

Blue Fox by Franz Marc

Try making your own paintings of animals using bright, unrealistic colors.

Elephant

Paint an oval body,
and add a trunk and legs.
In a different color, paint
a big ear, dot on an eye,
and add a tail.

Zebra

Paint a body and a neck.
Add a head, ears, four legs
and add a dab for a tail.

Crayon on some
stripes and a mane
in a different color.

Lion

Paint a round body and
four legs. In a darker
color, paint a round mane.
Add a head and ears on
top. Let the paint dry
and then crayon on
a face and tail.

Warm, cozy reds

Red paintings often look warm and inviting.
This artist used lots of reds and oranges to make
a bright, sunny painting of a bunch of flowers.

Flowers on a Red Ground by Marc Chagall

Use yellow, orange and red to make your own warm, cozy pictures.

Sun

Go around and around to paint a cheerful orange sun.

Add wavy shining rays.

Flower

Paint a big orange circle to make the middle of a flower. Paint pink petals coming out of it.

Happy hearts

Paint heart shapes in pinks and reds, and doodle some patterns on top.

Dab on some little yellow seeds.

Strawberries

To make strawberries, paint some heart shapes in red paint. Add some spiky green tops.

Cool, rainy blues

This artist used lots of watery blues to create
a splashy-looking picture of rain on a pond.

Rain by David Hockney

Blue pictures often look cool and calm. Try making
your own watery-looking pictures with blue paint.

Drips and splashes

To make a picture of splashy rain drops, cover your paper in water. Then dip a brush in runny paint and spatter it on top. Prop up the paper and allow it to drip-dry.

Painting with salt

Paint some blue fish on your paper. While the paint is still wet, scatter a few pinches of salt on top to look like scales.

Making waves

To paint waves, draw a rippling pattern in blue and white wax crayons, and then brush runny blue paint over the top.

Using Brushes

Artists use different-sized brushes and different brushstrokes to apply paint in lots of ways.

Sunset by Raoul Dufy

In this picture, the artist painted the sky with a wide brush, using big, broad brushstrokes. He used a thinner brush and wiggly brushstrokes to paint the waves.

22

Painting kites

Paint the sky with big, broad
brushstrokes, and then make a few
splotchy clouds by going around
and around with your brush.

Wait for the paint to dry, then add
diamond shapes with a thinner brush.
Use an even thinner brush, or
a felt-tip pen to add ribbons.

Pink flamingoes

Paint a flamingo body
and neck with a
medium-sized brush.
Use a thinner brush
to add two long legs
and a beak.

Add smoke
with big, swirly
brushstrokes.

Add windows with a black felt-tip pen when the paint is dry.

Steam train

To paint a picture of a steam train,
start by painting the sky and a hill
with big brushstrokes, then paint
a train with lots of carriages.

23

Tropical Jungle with Monkeys by Henri Rousseau

Squawk!

Jungle Prints

This artist painted a bright picture of monkeys in a tropical jungle. You can create your own jungle scene, using printing.

Use a finger to add dots in the middle.

For a flower, make several overlapping prints.

Leaf prints

To make a leaf print, brush thick paint over a leaf. Press it firmly onto paper.

Carefully peel off the leaf to leave a print.

Use different shapes
and sizes of leaves to fill
your jungle scene.

Flowers

Make lots of leaf
print flowers, long,
green stems and
curly vines.

Butterfly

Use a long, thin leaf to
print a body. Use a different
color to print four wings,
and then dot on two eyes
with a fingertip.

Bud

For a flower bud,
print three or four
overlapping petals.
Add a stem and a
leaf or two at the
bottom of the stem.

Parrot

Paint an oval body
and a round head, then
paint an eye and a beak.
Use long leaves to print
a tail, and wider leaves
to print wings.

Beetles

To make a beetle,
paint an oval.
Paint a line down
the middle, and dot
on eyes and spots.

Bugs

Paint a wiggly line.
Dot on an eye and
then add lots of legs.

Lines and circles

This painting is made up of colors, lines and circles. You can use printing to make pictures with lines and interesting shapes too.

Composition VIII by Wassily Kandinsky

Use household objects, such as bottle tops, the end of a pencil and pieces of cardboard to print different shapes and lines.

Mix some thick paint in a saucer. Dip in your object.

Then carefully press it onto paper to leave a print.

See what shapes you can make.

Strip of cardboard

pencil eraser

Curved cardboard

Shapes and circles

Print shapes and lines in
different colors to make
an interesting print.

Night owl

For an owl, use the end of a carrot
and a bottle top to print two eyes.
Use a piece of cardboard
to add a beak.

Use a small piece of cardboard
to print a zigzag pattern
for the tummy.

Bend pieces of cardboard into
curves for the body, wings and ears.

Sailboat

Use strips of cardboard to print a sailboat. Add stripes
or a skull and cross-bones to decorate your sails.

Ghost prints

This print is called a "ghost print," because the rabbits and leaves have been left blank. You can only see them because the background has been colored in.

Rabbit by William Morris

Follow these steps to make your own ghost prints.

Arrange some flat objects on paper. Stick them down with poster putty.

Dip a sponge in paint and dab it over them, then leave them to dry.

Carefully lift the objects to see their "ghosts."

Rabbit

To make a ghost rabbit, place two coins on your paper - one for a body, one for a head. Use a blob of poster putty for a tail, and add two leaves for ears.

Apple

Use a pipecleaner to make the outline of an apple shape. Use two blobs of poster tack for seeds, and a real leaf for the leaf.

Try using different objects and see what kinds of ghost prints they make.

Cutting and pasting

Some artists make pictures out of cut-out shapes. This is called collage.

The Parakeet and the Mermaid by Henri Matisse

Can you spot a parakeet and a mermaid in this picture?

snip
snip
snip
snip

Making cut-out shapes

Take a square piece of paper. Fold it in half.

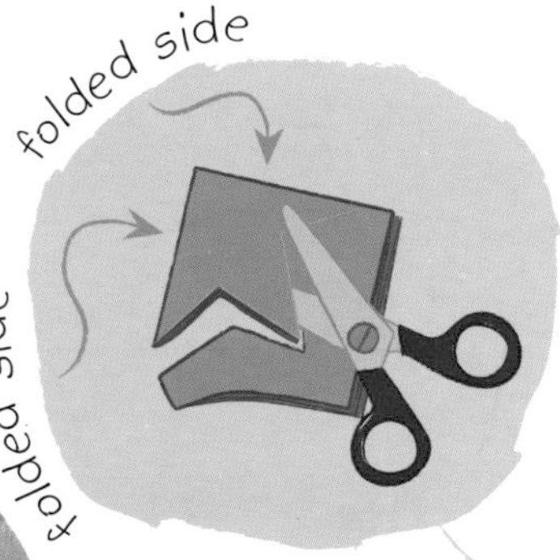

To make a star, fold the paper twice, like this. Cut out a pointy shape, like this.

folded side

folded side

Draw a shape along the fold. Cut it out.

folded side

Unfold the paper to see the finished star shape.

This artist painted paper and then cut out shapes with wiggly edges to make a person.

Carrot Nose by Jean Dubuffet

Spatter and splash

Splash paint onto paper to make interesting patterns for your cut-outs.

Bumble bee

Dip a brush in runny paint, and flick it over some paper.

Leave it to dry. Then, cut out a body and wings.

Cut out stripes, eyes and legs. Stick them onto the body.

Daisies

To make daisies, cut out yellow shapes for the middles, and add white petals around the edges.

High Sky 2 by Bridget Riley

Blocks and shapes

An artist named Bridget Riley used the same shapes again and again to create the bold, bright painting above. You could make something like it, using pieces of paper.

Patchwork shapes

Cut out lots of bright triangles, using colored paper or old magazines. See how many different ways you can arrange them.

Building blocks

Cut out blocks of different colors and paste them down next to each other.

Mixed shapes

Cut a mixture of circles and rectangles. Mix them together to make a pattern.

Woven pattern

Cut some long colored strips. Weave them over and under each other, like this.

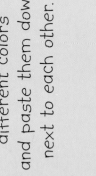

Ripping paper

These fish are made of pieces of broken up pottery from Ancient Egypt.

Glass fragments, Alexandria, Egypt

You can make an interesting looking "broken picture" by ripping up pieces of paper and putting them back together again.

Tear strips of green cardboard for the leaves.

To make a jigsaw picture, cut out a simple shape from some old gift wrap. Rip the shape up into a few pieces.

Put the pieces back together, leaving a space around each piece, then stick them down.

Paper trees

Rip a square shape for the leaves. Tear some long strips for the trunk and branches and stick them onto the square.

Crumbly castle

For a castle, rip a rectangle to make a tower, and some small squares for turrets. Add another rectangle to muke a window.

Pretty flowers

Rip up lots of little squares. Arrange the squares like this, to form a little flower.

Arrange lots of these together to make bigger flowers.

39

More paper ideas

Here are some things you can make using cut-outs and ripped paper.

Snowflakes

Fold a square piece of paper diagonally in half three times. Cut little holes into the edges. Then unfold it.

Houses

Mix up different shapes, such as squares, rectangles, and triangles to make a row of houses, like this.

Rain drop faces

Fold a small piece of paper in half and cut it in a curve shape to make a rain drop. Then cut two small holes for a nose and mouth.

Unfold it and draw on eyes.

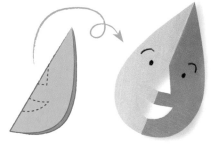

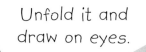

Butterfly

Fold a piece of paper in half, and cut out a shape like the letter B.

Unfold it and add a long piece of paper for the body.

Caterpillar

Tear lots of circle shapes and arrange them in a wiggly row to make a caterpillar shape.

Glue the shapes onto paper, and then draw on legs and feelers.

Ice cream

Tear three circles for ice cream scoops.

Cut out a tall triangle for a cone.

Cupcakes

Cut some little cake cases, and tear some rough triangle shapes for icing. Scrunch up small balls of tissue paper and stick them on top to make cherries.

Making models

Monkey and her Baby by Pablo Picasso

This monkey sculpture was put together using bits and pieces the artist found, including a toy car and a ball, and then cast in bronze.

Junk modeling

You can make models out of all kinds of objects. Wash and save old lids, pots, buttons, boxes... and anything else that you find interesting.

Junk robot

Glue different bits and pieces together to build up a figure.

Glue on colorful lids and pots to give your robot a face. You could make it smile or frown.

Cut out pieces of wrapping paper and glue them on to make feathers.

Rocking bird

Some artists make moving sculptures. You can make one too, by folding a paper plate in half. Paint the plate any color you like, and add an eye and a beak. Give it a push and then watch it rock back and forth.

More models

Some artists work with fabric. Artists Claes Oldenburg and Coosje van Bruggen made their soft viola out of cloth.

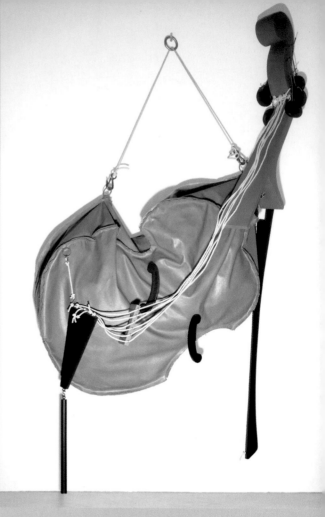

Soft Viola by Claes Oldenburg and Coosje van Bruggen

To make your own fabric sculpture, follow the steps below.

Fake cake

Stuff a sock with cotton stuffing. Wrap a rubber band around the end and cut off any extra fabric.

Wrap a rubber band around the toe of the sock to make a round cherry shape.

Cut out a strip of cardboard. Wrap it around the sock and stick it in place with tape.

An artist named Niki de Saint-Phalle made this huge, brightly colored sculpture.

You can make your own curvy sculptures using salt dough.

Charlotte by Niki de Saint-Phalle

Doughy shapes

To make a salt dough sculpture, follow the recipe on page 48.

Take a handful of salt dough. Roll or squeeze it into a shape.

Push your fingers into it to make holes.

Leave to harden. Paint when dry.

45

Turning one thing into another

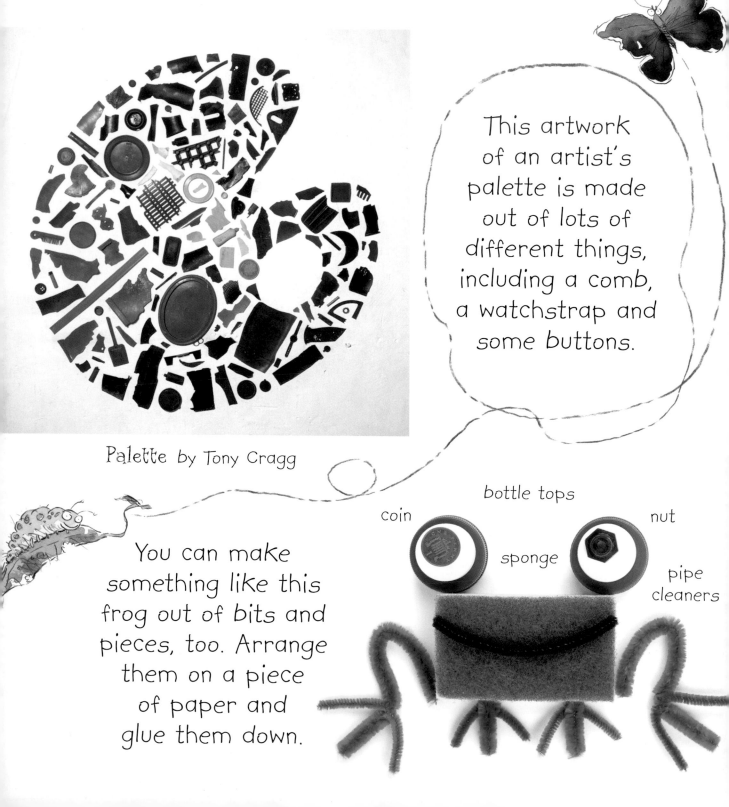

This artwork of an artist's palette is made out of lots of different things, including a comb, a watchstrap and some buttons.

Palette by Tony Cragg

You can make something like this frog out of bits and pieces, too. Arrange them on a piece of paper and glue them down.

coin

bottle tops

sponge

nut

pipe cleaners

Faces

Try making a face. It could be your own face, the face of an animal, a robot or an alien from outer space. You could use...

...Fruits (although you can't leave them lying around for long)...

...gift tags, paper clips, rubber bands...

...cookies and candies...

...leaves, twigs and flowers....

...or fabric, ribbons and buttons.

How to make salt dough

You will need:
2 cups of all-purpose flour
1 cup of table salt
1 cup of water

You could add:
One tablespoon of vegetable oil,
to make it easier to knead.

Put the flour and salt into a bowl, and slowly add the water, mixing it up to make soft dough.
If it's too sticky, add more flour. If it's too dry, add more water.
Put it on a flat surface, and knead it for ten minutes, until it's smooth.
Let it stand for twenty minutes before using it.
Dough can be stored in the refrigerator, or in clingfilm, for up to a week.

To dry...
You could leave it in the open air, which takes 3 to 4 days.
Or, bake it in an oven at around 200°F until it hardens.

Acknowledgements

Project artwork by Josephine Thompson, Antonia Miller and Katie Lovell
Project steps by Samantha Meredith, photography by Howard Allman
Photographic manipulation by Nick Wakeford
Picture research by Ruth King and Sam Noonan
Edited by Jane Chisholm and Jenny Tyler
Art Director: Mary Cartwright

p4 People at Night, Guided by Phosphorescent Tracks of Snails by Joan Miró © Succession Miro/ADAGP, Paris and DACS, London 2010/Philadelphia Museum of Art/CORBIS. **p6** An Elephant, a drawing Rembrandt van Rijn © The Trustees of the British Museum. **p8** Meduse by Alexei Von Jawlensky © DACS 2010, photo © White Images/Scala, Florence. **p10** Four Ballerinas on Stage by Edgar Degas © The Gallery Collection/Corbis. **p12** Yarl Jukurrpa (Bush Potato Dreaming) by Victor Jupurrula Ross © 2000 Victor Jupurrula Ross/DACS 2010/Courtesy Warlukurlangu Artists Aboriginal Corporation/British Museum, thanks to Beatriz Waters. **p16** Blue Fox, 1911 by Franz Marc, Van der Heydt Museum, Wuppertal, Germany/The Bridgeman Art Library. **p18** Flowers on a Red Ground by Marc Chagall © ADAGP, Paris and DACS, London 2010, image © Scala, Florence. **p20** Rain by David Hockney, 1973, from the weather series, lithograph and screenprint, edition: 98, 39 × 30 1/2" © David Hockney/Gemini G.E.L, image courtesy British Council Collection. **p22** Sunset by Raoul Dufy, artwork © ADAGP, Paris and DACS, London 2010/Leeds Museums and Galleries (City Art Gallery) U.K, image © The Bridgeman Art Library. **p24** Tropical Jungle with Monkeys by Henri Rousseau © Barnes Foundation/SuperStock. **p28** Composition VIII by Wassily Kandinsky © ADAGP, Paris and DACS, London 2010, image © Summit Labs/SuperStock. **p30** Rabbit pattern printed fabric by William Morris, digital image © The Museum of Modern Art, New York/Scala, Florence. **p32** The Parakeet and the Mermaid by Henri Matisse © Succession H Matisse/DACS 2010, image © Stedelijk Museum, Amsterdam. **p34** Carrot nose by Jean Dubuffet © ADAGP, Paris and DACS, London 2010/Scala, Florence. **p36** High Sky 2, 1992 by Bridget Riley © 2010 Bridget Riley, All rights Reserved. **p38** Glass Fragments © Werner Forman Archive/Scala, Florence. **p42** Monkey and her Baby by Pablo Picasso © Succession Picasso/DACS, London 2010/Musée Picasso, Paris, France/Giraudon/The Bridgeman Art Library. **p44** Soft Viola by Claes Oldenburg and Coosje van Bruggen, photo by Todd Eberle, courtesy the Oldenburg van Bruggen Foundation © 2002 Claes Oldenburg and Coosje van Bruggen. Charlotte by Niki de Saint Phalle, artwork © ADAGP, Paris and DACS, London 2010, image © akg-images/Dieter E. Hoppe. **p46** Palette by Tony Cragg, 1985, plastic materials, app. 210 × 240 cm, artwork © DACS 2010, photo by kind permission of Tony Cragg.